BEGINNING BLUES GU

Everything you need to know to become an accomplished performer of blues

&

Amsco Publications.

New York/London/Sydney/Cologne

This book is lovingly dedicated to my parents,
and to Janey, David, Nancy, Evic, Paolo, Heidi.
and my dear friend Nick.
Special thanks to Jason Shulman, Fred Sard,
and Herb Wise for their help and kindness.

Text photographs by Diana Davies (page 51), Ray Flerlage (pages 32, 54),
David Gahr (page 19), Mark Stein (pages 10, 14, 34, 35), Herbert Wise (page 7),
unknown (page 59).

International Standard Book Number: 0.8256.2350.2

Exclusive Distributors:
Music Sales Corporation
24 East 22nd Street, New York, NY 10010 USA
Music Sales Limited
8/9 Frith Street, London W1V 5TZ England
Music Sales Pty. Limited
120 Rothschild Street, Rosebery, Sydney, NSW 2018, Australia

Printed in the United States of America by
Vicks Lithograph and Printing Corporation

Contents

To the Student

Whether you are a beginning guitar student or a more experienced one, if you are interested in learning to play blues guitar in an authentic and exciting manner *How to Play Blues Guitar* has something for you.

In this book all aspects of blues guitar will be brought to light through the use of blues chords and scales, some really exciting licks, guided improvisations, and full-length solos. There are many fingerpicking lessons, and of course some classic blues songs by great artists such as Robert Johnson and Brownie McGhee, arranged so as to make use of all the techniques discussed in other pages.

As you can see, there is plenty of material to get involved with in this book. No matter what your goals may eventually be, I hope that the music on these pages will bring them closer to realization for you.

I'm sure you'll find that, whether you just want to improve your guitar-playing in general, or want to get started on becoming a "blues specialist," this book will contain exciting and useful lessons on *all* aspects of guitar-playing.

To the Teacher

I have made every effort to approach the contents of this book in a consistently authentic manner. Though almost all of the early blues players were entirely untutored in standard musical terms, I think it is possible to communicate their highly developed music in ways that are useful in a teaching situation. This book should serve as a guideline for the teacher, something he or she can embellish upon and present with that knowledge of an individual student only the teacher can have. For example, in my own teaching I stress improvisation as a learning technique. This form of self-discovery is ultimately one of the best ways to learn the blues. But just *when* to use this technique, and *how far* to go with it, are areas where your judgment and knowledge can be of unique help.

I hope both you and your students enjoy this book, and that it brings to them the same love of the blues I have found.

Reading Tablature and Symbols

Tablature

For those who cannot read music, *guitar tablature* is provided directly beneath all the standard music notation in this book. Tablature utilizes six horizontal lines which represent the six strings of the guitar, with the low E (or sixth) string at the bottom. On the right is an example of how it looks:

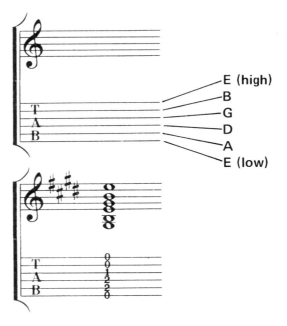

The numbers that appear on the lines of the tablature indicate the number of the fret at which your left hand holds down the string. This example shows how an open E chord would be represented:

Symbols

An arched line with an **s** over or under it connecting two notes indicates that your left hand *slides* to the second note with the same finger used for the first. As with the three following techniques (*hammer-on, pull-off,* and *bend*), the slide is a way of playing two notes while picking only the first note with the right hand.

If the arch has an **h** with it, this illustrates a *hammer-on*.

Here again, the right hand picks only the first note. The second is sounded by "hammering" with a left-hand finger *higher up* on the same string.

The same arch with a **p** represents a left-hand *pull-off*.

Here the second note, *lower down* on the string than the first, is "picked" with the left-hand finger which held the first note.

An arched line with a **b** means you *bend* the note. Here, you sound the second note by bending the string toward or away from you, bending with the left-hand finger which holds down the first note. In the example, the number or note in parentheses tied to the first note shows the note you will bend up to. You do not actually move to the fourth fret here, but, staying on the second fret, bend the string to sound a B. The first note is always quickly played, going immediately to the second, which is held the full time-value (𝅘𝅥𝅮.𝅘𝅥.𝅗𝅥.𝅗𝅥.).

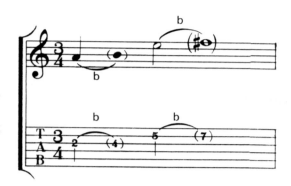

An **r** signals a *release* of a bend. This usually occurs right after a bend, returning to the original note.

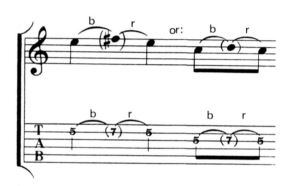

Sometimes a release will occur alone. Here, you bend the string *before* picking it with the right hand, so only the return sounds.

Note that when the bent note in parentheses has a *stem* going to the beam like the others, it has a time value equal to the others. The example here is played as a normal triplet:

Bending notes will be further explained in the section *Bending Strings*, p. 34.

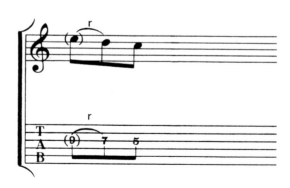

A straight line pointing up or down *toward* a note means you slide *to* that note from an optional point below or above it. A straight line pointing up or down *away* from a note means you slide *from* the note without going to another specific note with the slide.

A note played with *vibrato* will have a wavy line over it. *Vibrato* simply means to rapidly vibrate the left-hand in order to give the note a richer sound.

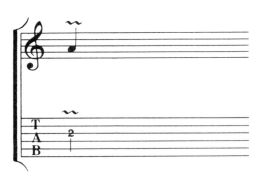

Pick direction is indicated as follows:
⊓ = downstroke
∨ = upstroke

The Pick

Guitar picks come in countless shapes, sizes, and thicknesses. Most guitarists have their own personal preferences, but if you are just starting out, it would be advisable to use a pick that is neither too small nor too large. I recommend using a medium-width pick, since it adapts itself more easily to all of the different possibilities encountered on the guitar.

The pick should be held between thumb and forefinger, and not gripped too tightly. The rest of the fingers on your picking hand should be in a relaxed position, halfway between being opened and closed.

All the pieces in this book should be played with the guitar pick ("flat-picking") unless otherwise indicated (there will be many fingerpicking pieces later on). It is important that you develop flexibility with the pick, and I recommend using alternating picking strokes (⊓ ∨ ⊓ ∨) as much as possible when practicing single-note playing. In some of the earlier exercises involving single-note work, I have indicated the picking strokes below the notes to give you a better idea of how the proper technique feels.

Blues Basics

It is important to become familiar with certain basics in blues guitar-playing before going on to more complicated material. A knowledge of blues chords and progressions, rhythm licks, and "turn-arounds" will give you the necessary tools to begin playing the blues.

The Blues Progression

The three main chords utilized in the blues are I, IV, and V. In the key of E these are: E, A, and B; in A: A, D, and E. The I chord (the *tonic*) takes its name from the first note of the scale in the key you are playing in. The IV, or *subdominant* chord, takes its name from the fourth note of the scale. The V, or *dominant* chord, takes its name from the fifth note of that scale.

I root (tonic)	IV sub-dominant	V dominant
A	D	E
B♭ (A♯)	E♭ (D♯)	F
B	E	F♯ (G♭)
C	F	G
D♭ (C♯)	G♭ (F♯)	A♭ (G♯·)
D	G	A
E♭ (D♯)	A♭ (G♯)	B♭ (A♯)
E	A	B
F	B♭ (A♯)	C
F♯ (G♭)	B	C♯ (D♭)
G	C	D
A♭ (G♯)	D♭ (C♯)	E♭ (D♯)

The Twelve-Bar Blues

The *twelve-bar blues* is the most well-known form of blues music for all instruments. Here is a twelve-bar blues progression in the key of E:

We will work in several keys throughout the course of this book, chiefly E, A, D, and G. Here are the many chord positions that should be known:*

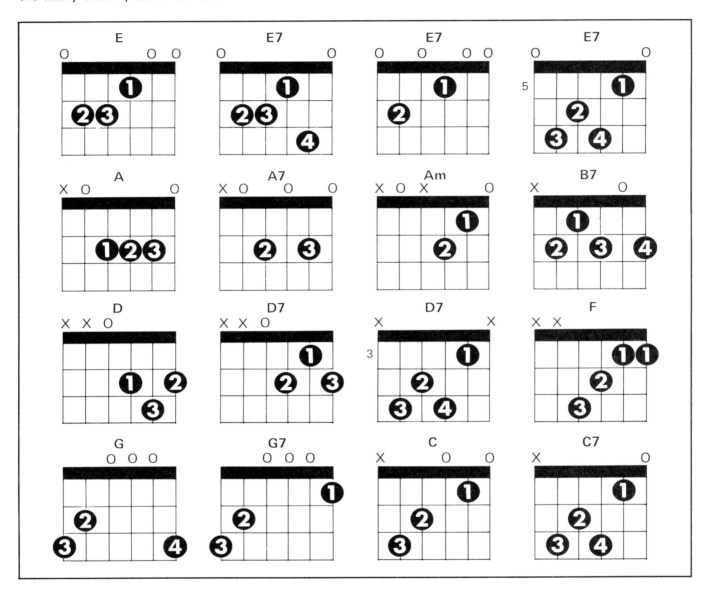

*Explanation of chord diagrams:

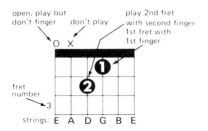

Barre Chords

Barre chords are among the most important tools the blues guitarist uses. They form the basis for many of the rhythmic licks in blues guitar-playing. Barre chords are chords where one finger is extended over a few or all of the strings, allowing the guitarist to move the chord up or down the fingerboard to any fret without changing the fingering. Here is an E-form barre chord:

G (E-form)

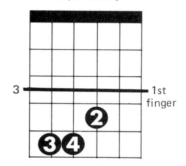

Here's the fingerboard with the names of the E-form barre chords corresponding to the frets. The "frets" are actually the metal bars across the fingerboard; but for our playing purposes when I say "fret" I mean the *space behind the bar*, where the fingers are held down.

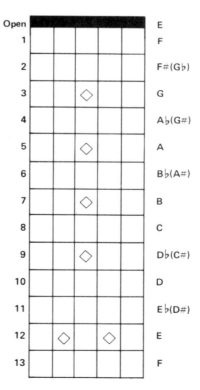

Rhythm Guitar

The Shuffle Rhythm

Before going on to learn the finer points of blues guitar-playing, it would be advisable to develop a good, solid foundation of rhythm techniques. The most familiar rhythm lick heard in blues rhythm guitar is called the *shuffle*. Everybody from Robert Johnson to Chuck Berry has used it, and here's what it looks like in the key of E*:

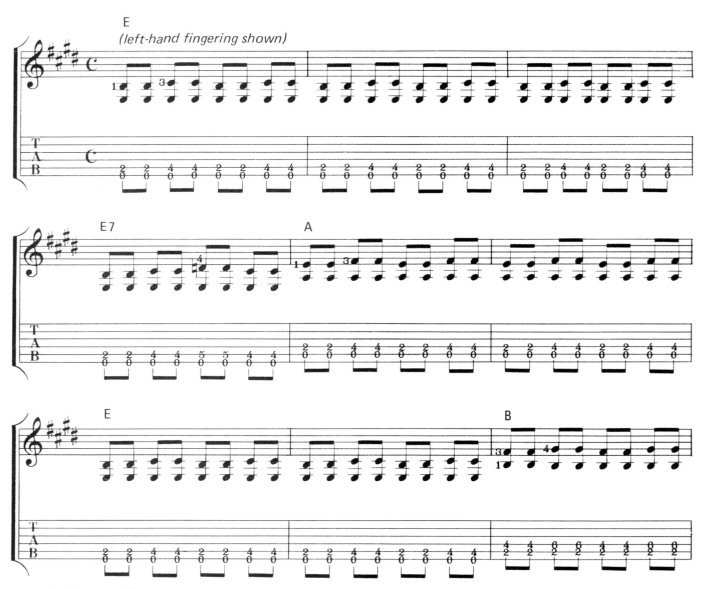

*Eighth notes (♪♪) in this book should always be played in shuffle rhythm (♪♪ or ♪♪), unless otherwise indicated.

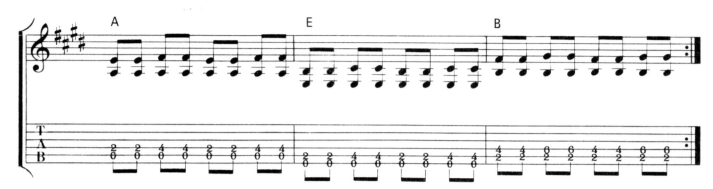

The next exercise is what I call the "harmony shuffle." It's the same lick as before, only this time you use four strings, with two of them moving in harmony with each other:

The Harmony Shuffle

*barre chord

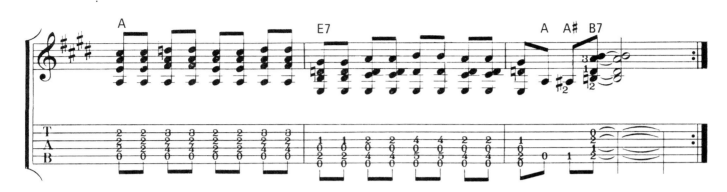

The shuffle-rhythm lick can also be played in other keys on the low E and A strings, using a position somewhat similar to that for barre chords. Here is an example of this way of playing it in the key of G:

The Shuffle Rhythm in G

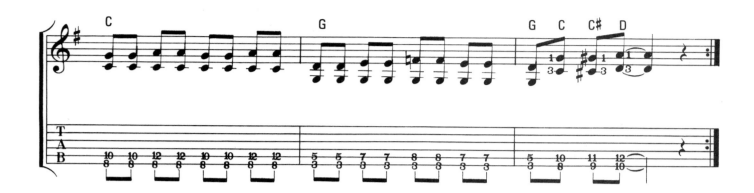

The harmony-shuffle lick illustrated two exercises ago can be played in many chord positions besides open E and A. The first new position is for D:

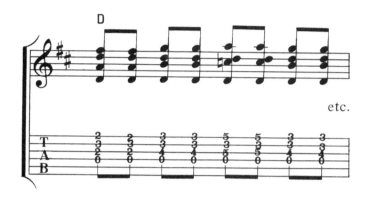

Below is the harmony shuffle for G. In this musical example the A (5th) string is left open but is not to be sounded. You can prevent it from sounding by damping it with the fingers of the left hand as they play the other notes. This is done by leaning the finger across the string so it does not vibrate, as shown here:

Note also that, for the third chord of the lick, the first finger of the left hand must come around to play the note G (third fret on the low E string), as in the photograph.

Here is the C chord position. In this exercise the D string must be damped.

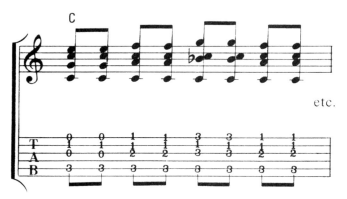

etc.

The Turnaround

The *turnaround* is a chord progression which takes place in the final two measures of the blues progression. It is called the "turnaround" because it actually serves to "turn the progression around", getting it back to the V, or dominant, chord before beginning again. Here is a diagram showing where the turnaround occurs, and what chords it involves in E:

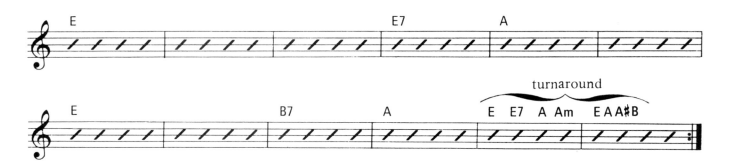

The next exercise is a harmony shuffle in the key of E; here the bass notes alternate with the rest of the chord. The last two bars use the turnaround as well. This rhythm lick is a good substitute sometimes for the straight shuffles you have been playing. In this exercise you will have to damp strings again: the D and G, at different times.

The Harmony Shuffle With Turnaround

Songs, of course, are the main expression of the blues. Working on some at this point will be extremely useful for putting into context some of the techniques you have learned, transforming the fragments into living blues sound. The first song is called *Good Morning Blues,** a tune that Sonny Terry and Brownie McGhee have performed. It is arranged for the key of E with a shuffle accompaniment and turnaround.

Good Mornin' Blues

Traditional. Arranged and adapted by Arlen Roth.

*For reasons of space it was possible to include only the first verse of each song. For complete verses to the songs in this book, see *Country Blues Songbook* (Oak Publications).

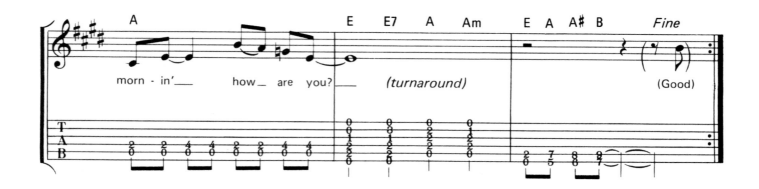

I've arranged this next song, Robert Johnson's classic, *Ramblin' On My Mind*, with a harmony shuffle accompaniment for the key of E. Note Johnson's use of an extra bar in E during the first measures, making a five-bar section in E and creating what is essentially a thirteen-bar progression.

Ramblin' On My Mind

Robert Johnson

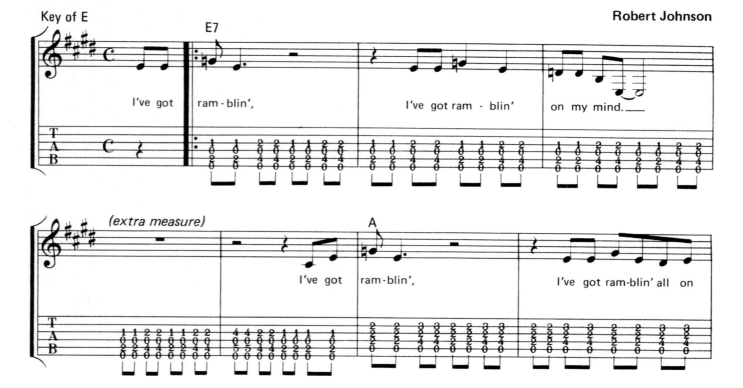

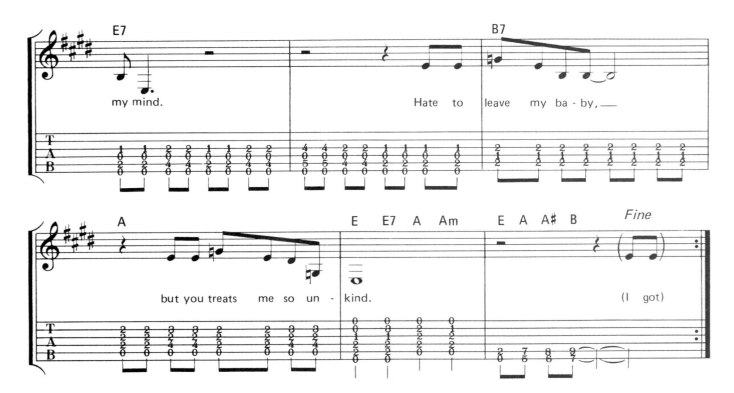

Fingerpicking Rhythms

Fingerpicking styles of playing are as essential a part of blues guitar as the "flat-picking" style you have been doing. For all applications of finger-picking I recommend an approach using the thumb and first three fingers. In this technique I employ the three fingers for the upper three strings: the ring finger for the high E, the middle finger for the B, and the index finger for the G string. The thumb should be used to sound the bass notes. If the particular lick you are playing covers other strings besides the highest three, your index, middle, and ring fingers should remain in the same relation to each other, only now covering those other strings. For example, if the lick used the B, G, and D strings, your ring finger would now cover the B, your middle finger the G, and your index finger would play the D string.

The Constant Bass

The *constant bass* is an important style of blues fingerpicking. Here is an exercise illustrating it for the key of E. Note that the rhythm the thumb plays is that of the shuffle lick which was covered earlier, this time using one note instead of two.

Son House

The Constant Bass

The Alternating Bass

The other main fingerpicking rhythm pattern is the *alternating bass* style. In playing this, the thumb moves back and forth between two strings to create a driving rhythm. The example below of the alternating bass is the only piece in this book not in shuffle rhythm. Eighth notes should be played as written (𝅘𝅥𝅮𝅘𝅥𝅮 = 𝅘𝅥𝅮𝅘𝅥𝅮).

The Alternating Bass

Lead Guitar: Scales, Licks, Solos

In this section I will discuss the three basic blues scale-patterns for lead playing. They are all based on the same scale, but each has a different range. They serve as a kind of foundation, since many runs and licks are based on them, and they apply to all keys.

Blues Pattern No. 1

The first blues pattern is the most widely used of all. Here it is in the key of A. To illustrate it in an open position, I've written it out for the key of E as well; in this position, of course, the fingering will be different.

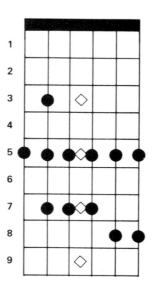

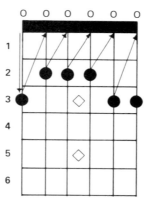

Blues Pattern No. 1—Key of E

E—Open Position

Blues Licks—Pattern No. 1

The following is a list of many useful licks that are derived from the blues scale you've just practiced. Please pay close attention to all of the subtleties incorporated in these riffs (slides, hammer-ons, pull-offs, etc.), for these techniques will help you to better understand the phrasing that is involved. The rhythm marked here is only a guideline; play the licks freely, in whatever rhythm feels right at the moment.

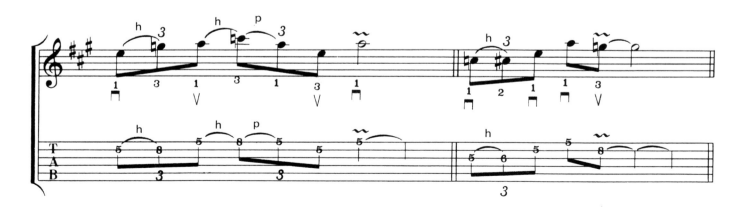

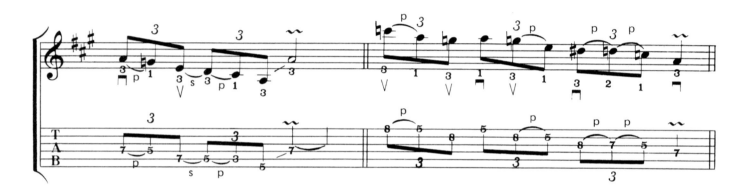

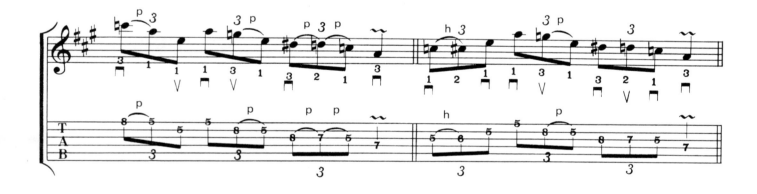

Blues Pattern No. 2

This pattern is quite similar to the first, since it begins with the same hand position. But it has a greater range and utilizes more of the fingerboard, therefore lending itself to more improvisational possibilities.

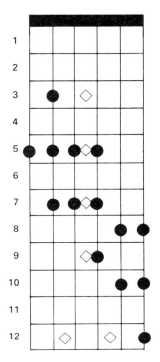

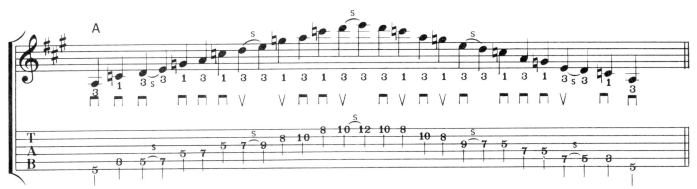

Blues Licks—Pattern No. 2

This next group of riffs is taken from our second blues scale-pattern. However, they are in the key of G, two frets down from A. You should be able to play all these licks in any key; this merely means starting on a different fret, of course. Note that the first lick in this exercise uses a note from Blues Pattern No. 1 (D on the second string). You eventually should be able to mix the patterns up freely.

Blues Licks—Pattern No. 2

Blues Pattern No. 3

Our third pattern begins with its root note (E) on the A string, as opposed to starting on the low E string as in the two previous ones. I have it written out here in E and also in A, much higher up on the fingerboard.

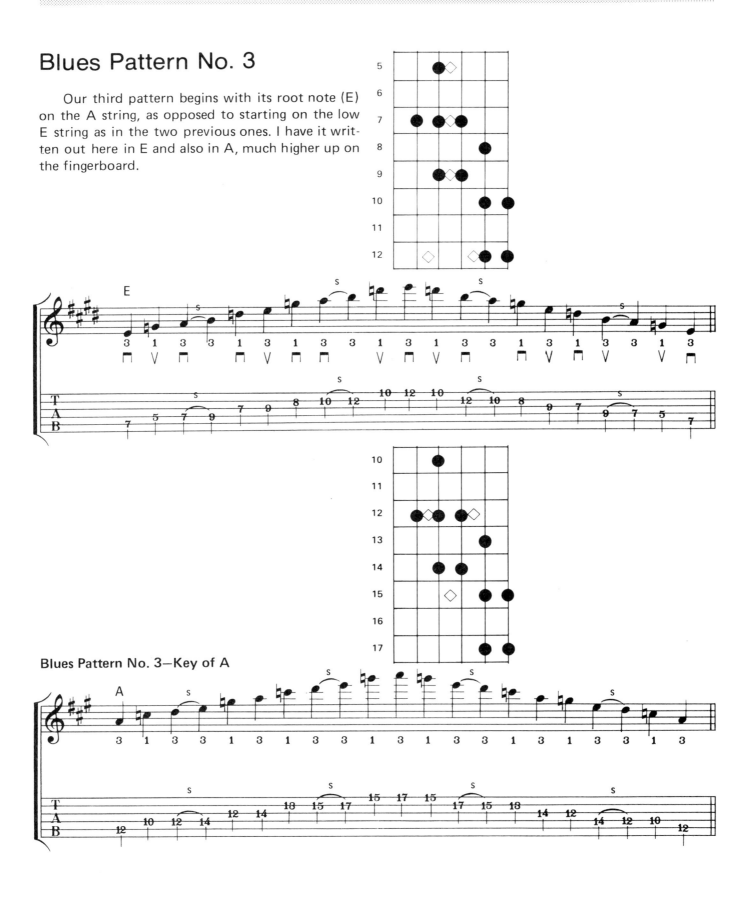

Blues Pattern No. 3—Key of A

Blues Licks—Pattern No. 3

These licks utilize the positions available within the third blues pattern. These are in the key of E:

Turnaround Licks

Whether you're playing lead guitar in a group or fingerpicking a solo blues piece, it's always nice to play an interesting lick during the turnaround. Of course, with the proper phrasing, almost any riff can be employed during these two bars. There are, however, some traditionally popular turnaround licks you should know first, and I've written them out here in both E and A to illustrate their open and closed positions:

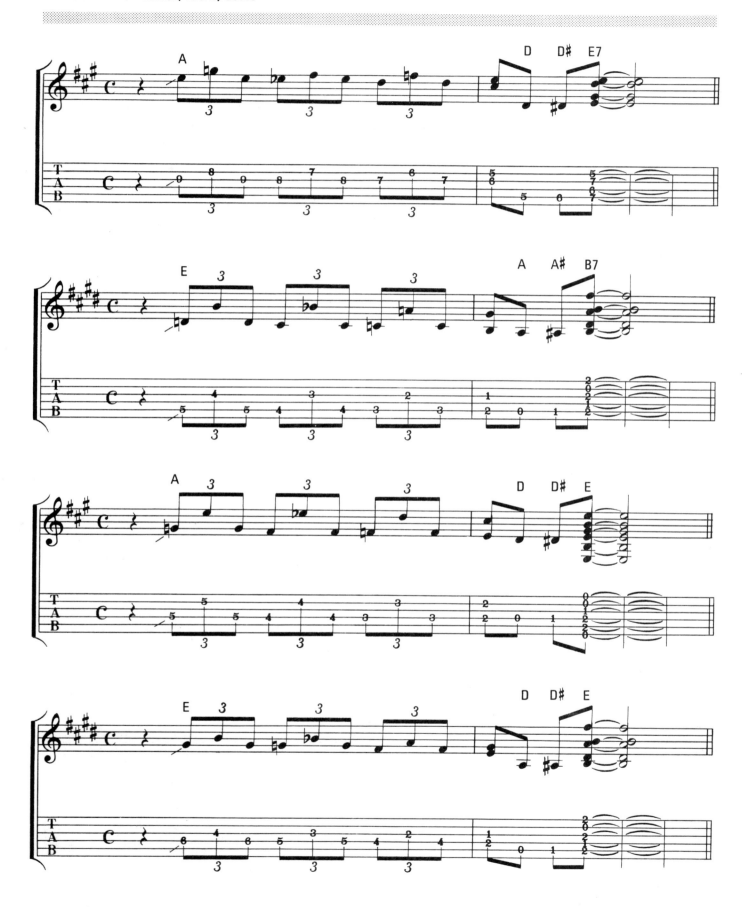

Now that some blues licks and turnaround licks are a part of the student's vocabulary, it would be good to try this famous Robert Johnson song. I've arranged it so you can use some of the licks as "fills" in the short instrumental passages between vocal lines. This is also the first song in this book to use a turnaround lick.

Crossroad Blues

Key of E

Robert Johnson

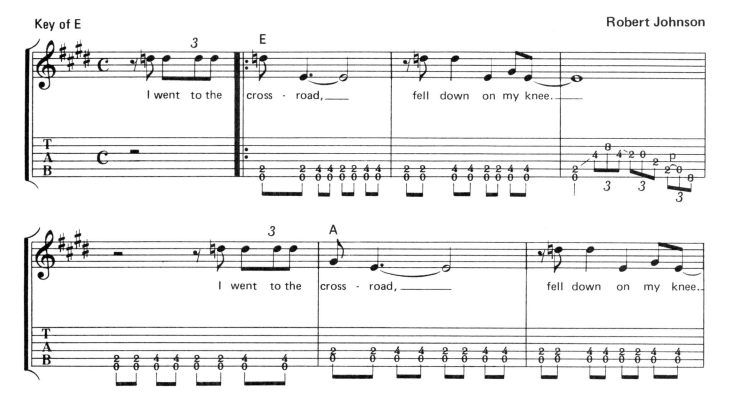

I went to the cross - road,_____ fell down on my knee._____

I went to the cross - road,_____ fell down on my knee.

I asked the Lord to have mer - cy, _____

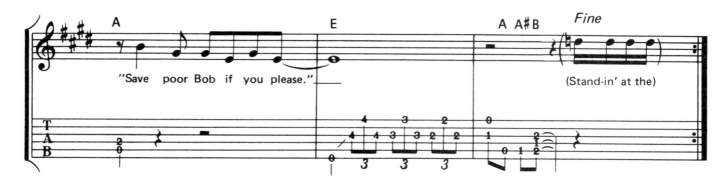

"Save poor Bob if you please." _____

Fine

(Stand-in' at the)

Dust My Broom is another great Robert Johnson song that was made quite famous in the 1950s by the important Chicago bluesman, Elmore James. The arrangement I've written out is a bit more complicated than the previous song, with more complex lead fills:

Buddy Guy

Dust My Broom

Key of E

Robert Johnson

I'm goin' to get up in the morn-ing, I be-lieve I'll dust my broom.

I'm goin' to get up in the morn-ing, I be-lieve I'll dust my broom.

Girl friend, the black man you been lov-in'

girl friend, can get my room.

(I'm gon-na)

Bending Strings

Another very important tool for the blues guitarist is the technique of *bending strings*. This is a way of changing pitch by pushing or pulling the string toward or away from you, rather than by moving to another fret.* The effect is somewhat like a slide. This technique adds to the subtle emotional qualities of the blues, because it utilizes something truly exclusive to string instruments: the ability to sound unwritten notes that actually are there *between half-steps* (guitar frets are a half-step apart).

How To Bend

Generally, the outer strings should be bent toward the middle of the fingerboard; that is, the highest two strings (E and B) *pushed* toward you, and the lowest two *pulled* away from you. Occasionally, however, the way a lick is fingered will make this so awkward that you will have to ignore this rule.

Before actually playing bending licks, I think one should be technically adept at the physical act of bending strings. A frequent mistake is bending a string with only one finger, thereby getting a weak attack to the bend and not having the strength to maintain the note once the string is stretched. Therefore, when bending a string, always help your finger along with as many of the other fingers as are available behind it. In the photographs of strings being bent by the ring and middle fingers, note the positioning of the other fingers helping to bend the string:

> *Note*: I should also mention that if you are playing a steel-string acoustic guitar, you should only attempt bending with light-gauge strings at the heaviest. But whether playing acoustic guitar or electric (which can handle much lighter strings), don't try to bend the G string too far, unless it is of the unwound variety. If one of the riffs given here indicates a two-fret bend on the G string and you're practicing with a wound G, a one-fret bend will suffice.

*This was discussed in the first section of this book, *Reading Tablature and Symbols.*

Bending with the ring finger

B string—Push

G string—Pull

Bending with the middle finger

G string—Push

Almost all of the bends that follow involve either the *sevenths* or *fourths* of the keys you are playing in. For example, in the key of E you can bend on all the D notes (7th) or the A notes (4th). The sevenths are bent up to the root note, and the fourths are bent up to the fifth. Here are the three blues patterns illustrated earlier, with circles around the possible notes to be bent.

Bending with the middle finger

G string—Pull

Blues Pattern No. 1

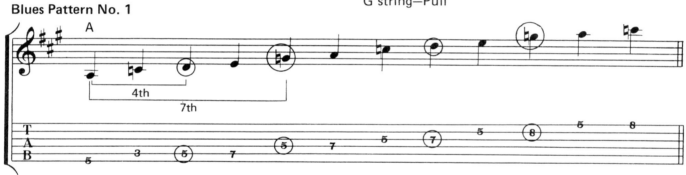

Blues Pattern No. 2

Blues Pattern No. 3

Here, now, are some bending licks that should be well-practiced:

Bending Licks

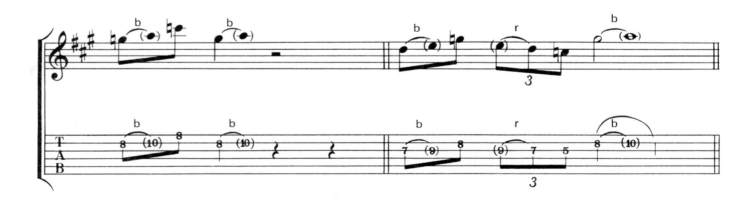

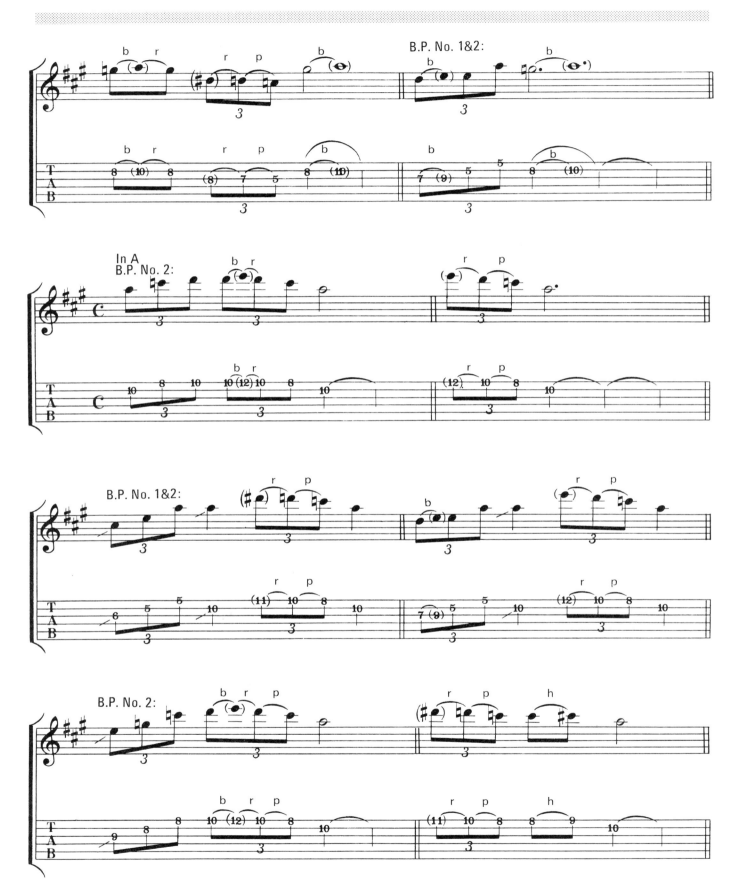

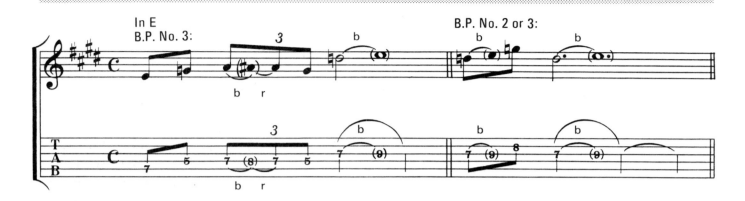

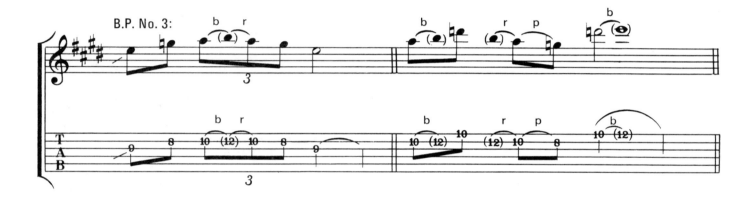

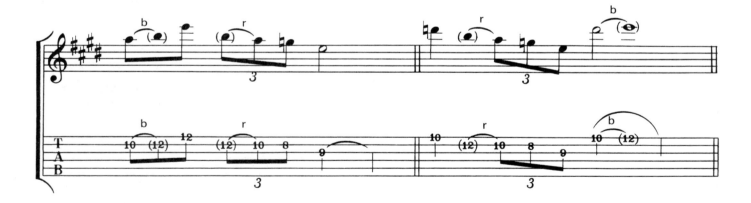

Blues Solos

The next six exercises are twelve-bar blues progressions combining both the rhythm and lead techniques that have been discussed in the previous pages. They can be practiced alone, but the accompaniment of a teacher, friend, or prerecorded rhythm-guitar part might help you to achieve a smoother, more even rhythm in your playing.

Blues Solos

This arrangement of Robert Johnson's *When You Got a Good Friend* will be using some licks that involve bending strings. The act of playing complex fills and coming out of them cleanly and on the right beat is a difficult one, so it might take some time and practice before it really begins to happen.

When You Got A Good Friend

Robert Johnson

Here's a song that was written and recorded by Bo Weevil Jackson. It's the first song in this book in the key of A:

You Can't Keep No Brown

Bo Weevil Jackson

Here's another arrangement in the key of A,
Future Blues by Willie Brown.

Future Blues

Key of A

Willie Brown

This song by Marshall Owens is arranged for the key of D.

Texas Blues

Marshall Owens

This moving Robert Johnson song utilizes an unusual fourteen-bar format. It is written here in the key of G.

If I Had Possession Over Judgment Day

Key of G

Robert Johnson

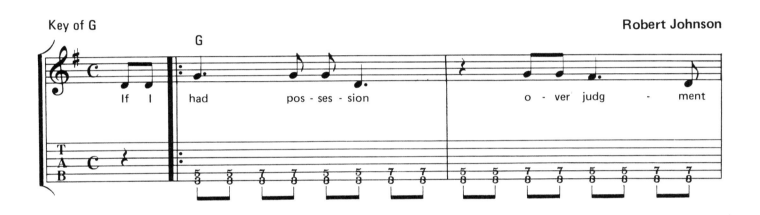

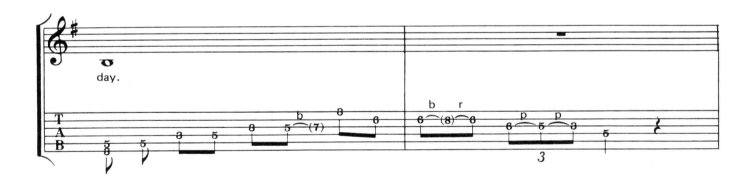

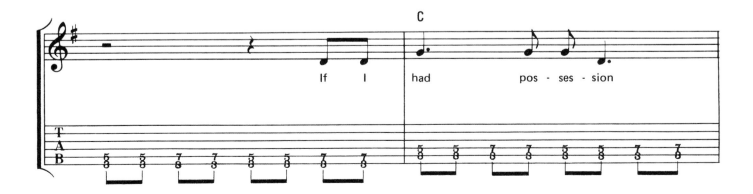

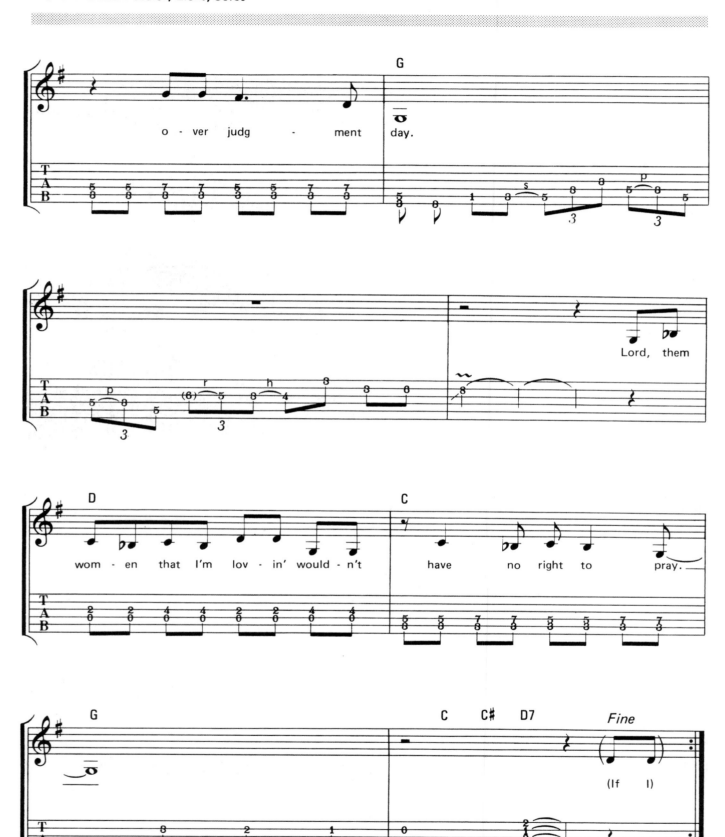

Fingerpicking the Blues

Fingerpicking is probably the oldest form of blues guitar-playing. The best examples of this art-form have always been by blues singers accompanying themselves in a solo effort. The 1920's and '30's produced the best recorded works by blues fingerpickers, and if you are interested in this style I strongly recommend picking up some of these recordings. Many of these important records are listed in the discography in the back of this book.

As I discussed earlier in the book, the two most widely used fingerpicking styles are the *constant bass* and the *alternating bass*. All of the songs and exercises in this chapter will utilize these two techniques; throughout all the pieces you should concentrate on maintaining the three-fingered approach I mentioned earlier.*

Jess Fuller

Fingerpicking Licks

Before getting into playing actual fingerpicking tunes, the student should first become fairly accustomed to playing in the style. Here, then, are some new blues licks with the right-hand fingering written below the tablature. **1** signifies the index finger, **2** the middle finger, and **3** means the ring finger. **T** means the note is played with the thumb.

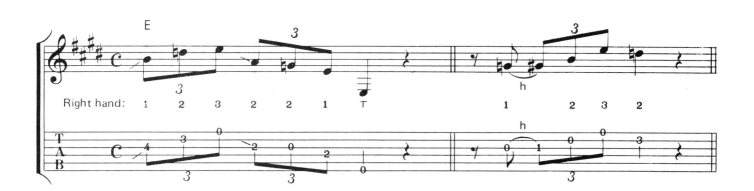

*Described in detail on p. 19.

Turnaround Licks
Fingerpicking Style

Here are some turnaround licks, both familiar and new, in fingerpicking style, coupled with a constant shuffle bass played by the thumb:

Fingerpicking Solos

This next group of constant-bass exercises begins fairly simply and becomes more complex as it goes along. You will need to use much concentration and practice in order to develop a *clean separation between the bass and lead notes,* essential to this style of playing.

Otis Rush

Fingerpicking Solos

Fingerpicking Tunes

The next three songs are arranged for blues fingerpicking, and they utilize just about every technique that has been discussed in this book. You should always remember that if you really feel confident, you shouldn't hesitate to begin to improvise. This *art of improvisation* is what will really begin to open up a whole new world for the blues guitarist.

This song in the key of E was written by Blind Joe Reynolds. *Cream* recorded a popular version of it on their first album.

B. B. King

Outside Woman Blues

Key of E

Blind Joe Reynolds

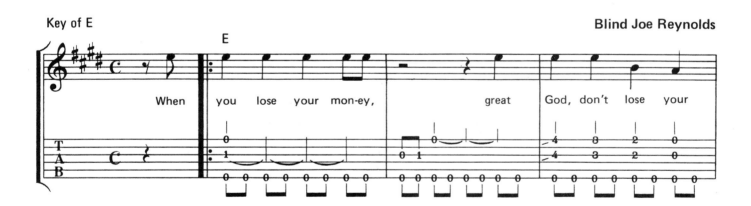

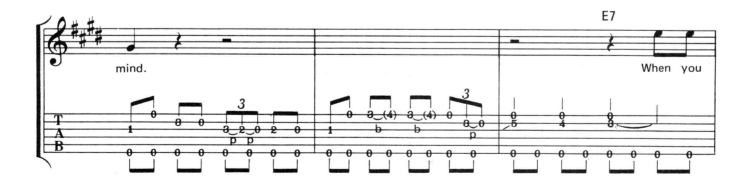

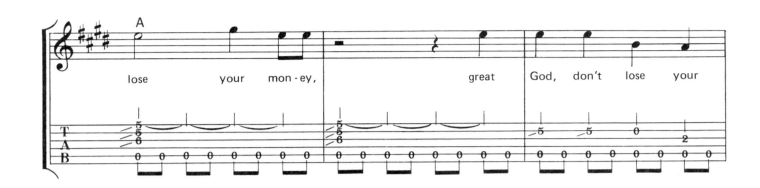

lose   your   mon-ey,   great God, don't   lose   your

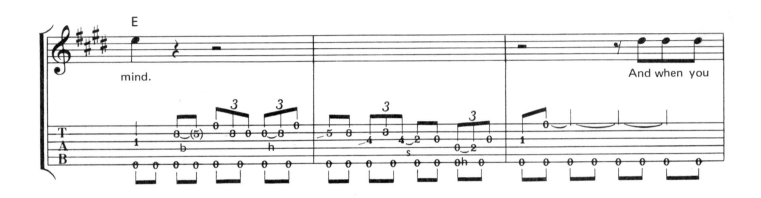

mind.   And when you

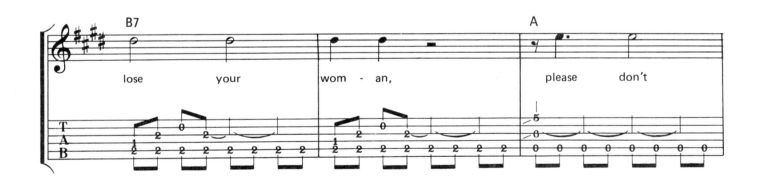

lose   your   wom - an,   please   don't

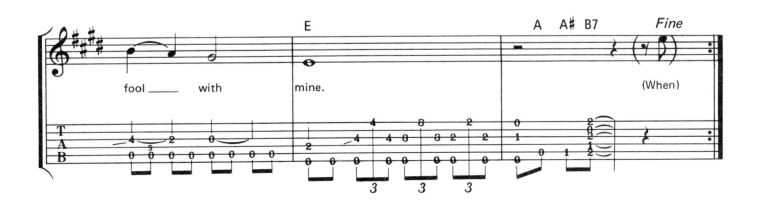

fool ____ with   mine.   (When)

Walkin' Blues was written and first recorded by Robert Johnson. As is the case with so many of his songs, other artists have since recorded countless versions of it. Here it is in the key of A.

Walkin' Blues

Key of A

Robert Johnson

Another great Johnson song, *Travelin' Riverside Blues*, is written here with a constant-bass accompaniment that consists simply of four straight quarter-notes per bar, rather than eighth notes (as in the constant shuffle bass).

Travelin' Riverside Blues

Key of E

Robert Johnson

In Conclusion

Playing blues guitar can be a very rewarding experience—each note that you learn as you progress can be a thrill in itself. I hope that the music you've been playing in this book has helped you to begin speaking the special language of the blues. I would advise continuing your development by improvising more with the licks and progressions you know, playing with other musicians, and listening to as many blues recordings as you can.

I sincerely hope that this book is just a beginning for you in your development into a fine blues guitarist.

Discography

Here are some blues recordings that I would recommend a new student of blues guitar pick up on:

Traditional Folk Blues
Robert Johnson/*King of the Delta Blues Singers* (volumes 1 and 2), Columbia CL1654, C30045
Son House/*Father of Folk Blues*, Columbia CS9217
Charley Patton/*Founder of the Delta Blues,* Yazoo L1020
Blind Willie McTell/*1927-1933, The Early Years,* Yazoo, L1005
Blind Blake/*Search Warrant Blues* (vols. 1 and 2), Biograph 12003, 12023
Guitar Wizards, 1926-1935, Yazoo L1016
Mississippi Moaners, 1927-1942, Yazoo L1009
Bo Carter, Greatest Hits 1930-1940, Yazoo L1014
Mississsippi John Hurt, Vanguard 19/20

Lead Guitar—Electric Blues
B.B. King/*Completely Well*, Bluesway BLS 6037
Elmore James, John Brim/*Whose Muddy Shoes,* Chess 1537
Albert King, Otis Rush/*Door to Door,* Chess 1538
T-Bone Walker/*Stormy Monday Blues*, Bluesway BLS 6008.
Buddy Guy/*A Man and the Blues*, Vanguard VSD 79272
Chicago/*The Blues Today* (vols. 1, 2 and 3), Vanguard VSD 79216, 79217, 79218